JOHN W. SCHAUM
RHYTHM SPELLER

2

Contents

TEACHER'S MEMO: Be sure to read "How to Use the Rhythm Speller" on page one. Also no that there is a removable answer section in the front of the book.

3

LESSON 1
Note and Rest Refresher

Notes and rests get their names from fractions. Study the following **chart.**

WHOLE															
$\frac{1}{2}$								$\frac{1}{2}$							
$\frac{1}{4}$				$\frac{1}{4}$				$\frac{1}{4}$				$\frac{1}{4}$			
$\frac{1}{8}$		$\frac{1}{8}$		$\frac{1}{8}$		$\frac{1}{8}$		$\frac{1}{8}$		$\frac{1}{8}$		$\frac{1}{8}$		$\frac{1}{8}$	
$\frac{1}{16}$	$\frac{1}{16}$	$\frac{1}{16}$	$\frac{1}{16}$	$\frac{1}{16}$	$\frac{1}{16}$	$\frac{1}{16}$	$\frac{1}{16}$	$\frac{1}{16}$	$\frac{1}{16}$	$\frac{1}{16}$	$\frac{1}{16}$	$\frac{1}{16}$	$\frac{1}{16}$	$\frac{1}{16}$	$\frac{1}{16}$

Part I

DIRECTIONS: On the blank diagram below, write NOTES to fill each of the sections. Thus in section "a", you will write one whole note. In sections "b", you will write two half notes, (one in each section), etc. When you get to sections "e", draw in 16 sixteenth notes.

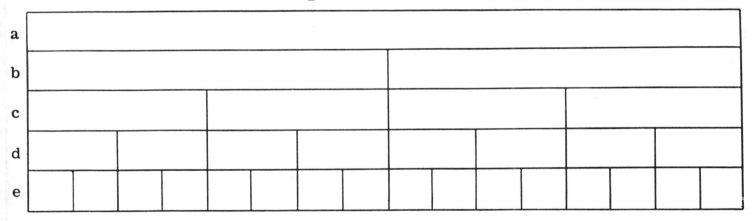

Part II

DIRECTIONS: On the blank diagram below, write RESTS in every section.

LESSON 2

A Whole and Its Parts (Notes)

DIRECTIONS: Each of the following diagrams represent a WHOLE. The dividing lines separate the diagrams into either halves, quarters, eighths, or sixteenths. You are to fill the sections of each diagram with the right kind of notes. When no dividing lines are present, insert a whole note.

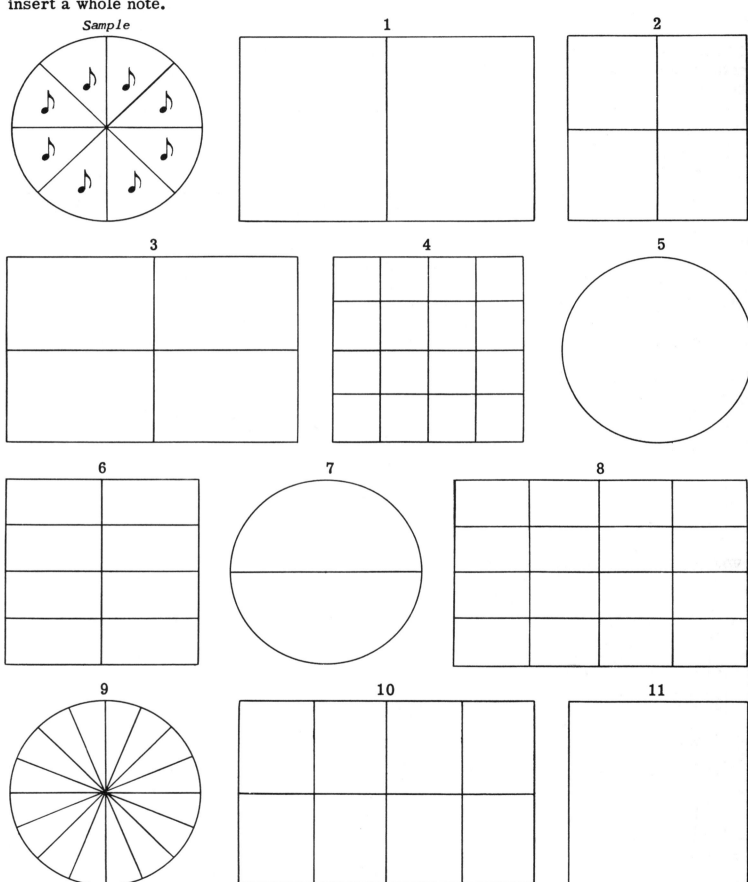

Sample

1

2

3

4

5

6

7

8

9

10

11

LESSON 3
Information Please
(Note Values)

Part I

DIRECTIONS: On each of the dotted lines, write a number which gives the correct amount of notes that are equal to the first part of each problem. Use the diagrams of Lesson Two to help you.

Sample

1. ♩ = ..2.. ♩
2. o = ... ♩
3. o = ... ♪
4. o = ... ♩
5. o = ... ♪
6. ♩ = ... ♪
7. 2 ♩ = ... ♩
8. 2 ♩ = ... ♪
9. ♩ = ... ♪
10. 2 ♩ = ... ♪

11. ♩ = ... ♪
12. 3 ♩ = ... ♪
13. 4 ♩ = ... ♪
14. 2 ♩ = ... ♪
15. ♩ = ... ♪
16. 4 ♩ = ... ♪
17. 3 ♩ = ... ♪
18. 2 ♩ = ... ♪
19. ♪ = ... ♪
20. 2 ♪ = ... ♪

21. 5 ♪ = ... ♪
22. 4 ♪ = ... ♪
23. 3 ♪ = ... ♪
24. 8 ♪ = ... ♪
25. 7 ♪ = ... ♪
26. 6 ♪ = ... ♪
27. 16 ♪ = ... o
28. 8 ♪ = ... o
29. 4 ♩ = ... o
30. 2 ♩ = ... o

Part II

Which is longer? Draw a line around the part that is longer.

Sample

1. ♩ ♩ or (o)
2. ♩ or ♬♬
3. ♫ or ♪
4. ♫ or ♫
5. ♪ ♪ or ♩
6. o or ♩ ♩ ♩
7. ♩ or ♪ ♪
8. ♪ ♪ ♩ or ♩
9. ♫ ♩ or ♩ ♩
10. ♩ ♪ or ♫ ♪
11. ♫♫ or ♩
12. ♩ ♫ ♩ or o
13. ♪ ♪ ♪ or ♩
14. ♩ ♩ ♩ or ♫ ♩ ♪
15. ♩ ♪ ♪ or ♪ ♩

LESSON 4
An Arithmetic Lesson in Notes

DIRECTIONS: Write each answer in ONE note.

ADDITION

Sample

1. ♪ + 𝅗𝅥 + ♩ = ...♩... (Sample)

2. ♫ + 𝅗𝅥 = ...

3. 𝅗𝅥 + ♩ + ♫ = ...

4. 𝅗𝅥 + ♪ = ...

5. ♪ + ♬ + ♩ = ...

6. ♪ + 𝅗𝅥 = ...

7. ♬ + ♪ + ♩ + ♩ = ...

8. ♪ + ♪ + ♬ = ...

9. 𝅗𝅥 + ♩ + 𝅗𝅥 = ...

10. ♫ + ♬ + ♩ = ...

MULTIPICATION

Sample

1. ♪ × 2 = ...♩... (See Lesson 3, Part 1, No. 11)

2. 𝅗𝅥 × 4 = ...   ditto   No. 4

3. ♪ × 8 = ...   ,,   No. 9

4. ♩ × 2 = ...   ,,   No. 2

5. ♪ × 4 = ...   ,,   No. 6

6. 𝅗𝅥 × 2 = ...   ,,   No. 19

7. ♩ × 2 = ...   ,,   No. 1

8. 𝅗𝅥 × 8 = ...   ,,   No. 3

9. ♪ × 4 = ...   ,,   No. 15

10. 𝅗𝅥 × 16 = ...   ,,   No. 5

SUBTRACTION

Sample

1. 𝅝 - ♩ = ...♩... (Sample)

2. ♩ - ♪ = ...

3. 𝅗𝅥 - ♫ = ...

4. 𝅗𝅥 - ♬ = ...

5. ♪ - ♪ = ...

6. 𝅝 - 𝅗𝅥 𝅗𝅥 = ...

7. ♩ - 𝅗𝅥 = ...

8. 𝅗𝅥 - ♬♬ = ...

9. ♩ - ♪ ♪ = ...

10. ♩ - ♪ ♪ = ...

DIVISION

Sample

1. ♩ ÷ 2 = ... (See Lesson 3, Part 1, No. 11)

2. 𝅝 ÷ 2 = ...   ditto   No. 2

3. 𝅗𝅥 ÷ 2 = ...   ,,   No. 1

4. 𝅝 ÷ 8 = ...   ,,   No. 3

5. 𝅗𝅥 ÷ 2 = ...   ,,   No. 19

6. ♩ ÷ 4 = ...   ,,   No. 6

7. 𝅝 ÷ 4 = ...   ,,   No. 4

8. 𝅗𝅥 ÷ 8 = ...   ,,   No. 9

9. 𝅝 ÷ 16 = ...   ,,   No. 5

10. 𝅗𝅥 ÷ 4 = ...   ,,   No. 15

A Whole and Its Parts (Rests)

DIRECTIONS: Each of the following diagrams is a WHOLE, The dividing lines separate the diagrams into either halves, quarters, eighths, or sixteenths. You are to fill each diagram with the right kind of rests. When no dividing lines are present, insert a whole rest.

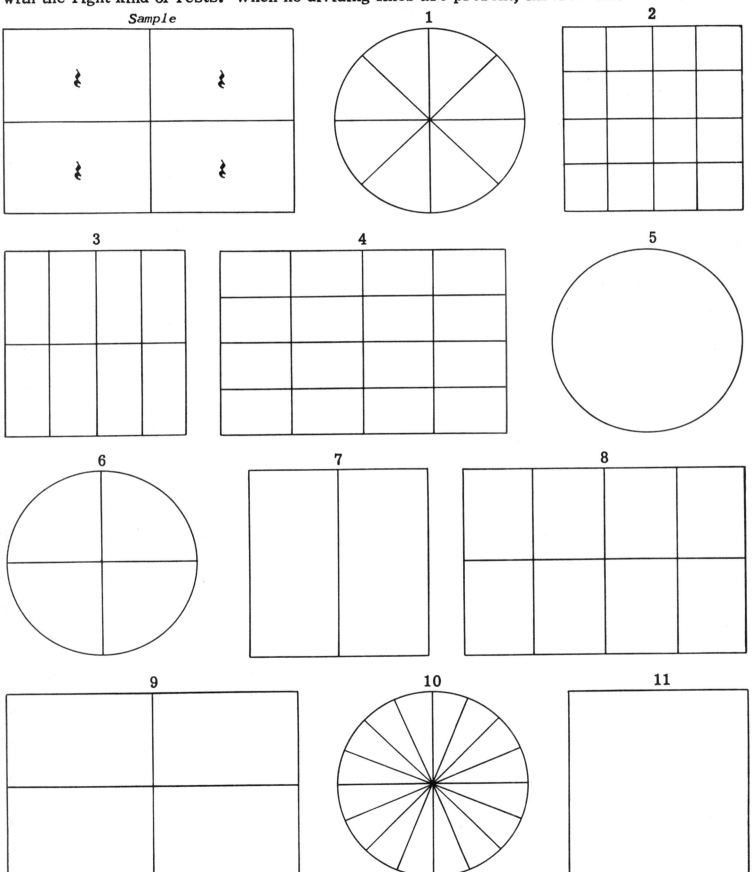

LESSON 6
Information Please
(Rest Values)

Part I

DIRECTIONS: On each dotted line, write the number which gives the correct amount of rests needed to equal the first part of each problem. Use the diagrams of Lesson Five to help you.

1. ▬ = ...2... ≀ (Sample)   11. 2 ▬ = ... 𝄾   21. 6 𝄾 = ... 𝄿

2. ▬ = ... 𝄾   12. 3 ≀ = ... 𝄾   22. 𝄾 = ... 𝄿

3. ▬ = ... ▬   13. 2 ≀ = ... 𝄾   23. 5 𝄾 = ... 𝄿

4. ▬ = ... 𝄿   14. 4 ≀ = ... 𝄾   24. 3 𝄾 = ... 𝄿

5. 2 ▬ = ... ≀   15. ≀ = ... 𝄿   25. 8 𝄾 = ... 𝄿

6. ▬ = ... 𝄿   16. 3 ≀ = ... 𝄿   26. 7 𝄾 = ... 𝄿

7. ▬ = ... 𝄾   17. 4 ≀ = ... 𝄿   27. 2 ▬ = ... ▬

8. 2 ▬ = ... 𝄾   18. 2 ≀ = ... 𝄿   28. 8 𝄾 = ... ▬

9. ▬ = ... ≀   19. 2 𝄾 = ... 𝄿   29. 16 𝄿 = ... ▬

10. ≀ = ... 𝄾   20. 4 𝄾 = ... 𝄿   30. 4 ≀ = ... ▬

Part II

Which is longer? Draw a line around the part that is longer.

1. ▬ or (≀ ≀ ≀)   6. ≀ 𝄿 or 𝄾 𝄾 𝄾   11. 𝄾 ≀ 𝄿 𝄿 or 𝄾 ▬

2. ≀ 𝄾 or ≀ 𝄿 𝄿 𝄿   7. ▬ or ▬ ≀   12. ≀ 𝄾 or 𝄾 𝄾 𝄿

3. 𝄿 ≀ or ▬   8. 𝄿 𝄾 ≀ or ≀ ≀   13. ▬ or ≀ 𝄾 𝄾 𝄾

4. ▬ or ≀ ≀ 𝄾 ▬   9. ≀ ≀ ≀ ≀ or ▬ 𝄾 𝄾   14. ▬ ≀ or ▬ ▬

5. 𝄾 𝄾 or 𝄿 𝄿   10. ▬ or ≀ ≀ ▬ ≀   15. 𝄾 𝄾 𝄾 or ≀ 𝄾

LESSON 7
An Arithmetic Lesson in Rests

DIRECTIONS: Write each answer in ONE rest.

ADDITION

(Sample)

1. 𝄻 + 𝄾 𝄾 = ...𝄼....
2. 𝄾 𝄾 + 𝄾 = ...
3. 𝄾 + 𝄾 = ...
4. 𝄾 + 𝄾 = ...
5. 𝄻 + 𝄻 = ...
6. 𝄾 𝄾 + 𝄾 = ...
7. 𝄾 𝄾 + 𝄾 𝄾 = ...
8. 𝄾 𝄾 + 𝄻 + 𝄾 = ...
9. 𝄾 𝄾 𝄾 𝄾 + 𝄾 = ...
10. 𝄾 + 𝄾 = ...

MULTIPICATION

(Sample)

1. 𝄾 × 2 = ...𝄼.... (See Lesson 6, Part I, No. 1)
2. 𝄾 × 8 = ...   ditto   2
3. 𝄾 × 4 = ...   ,,   9
4. 𝄾 × 2 = ...   ,,   22
5. 𝄾 × 8 = ...   ,,   6
6. 𝄻 × 2 = ...   ,,   3
7. 𝄾 × 4 = ...   ,,   15
8. 𝄾 × 2 = ...   ,,   10
9. 𝄾 × 16 = ...   ,,   4
10. 𝄾 × 4 = ...   ,,   7

SUBTRACTION

(Sample)

1. 𝄾 − 𝄾 = ...𝄾....
2. 𝄼 − 𝄾 𝄾 = ...
3. 𝄻 − 𝄾 = ...
4. 𝄾 − 𝄾 𝄾 = ...
5. 𝄼 − 𝄻 = ...
6. 𝄾 − 𝄾 = ...
7. 𝄾 − 𝄾 𝄾 = ...
8. 𝄻 − 𝄾 𝄾 = ...
9. 𝄼 − 𝄾 𝄾 𝄾 = ...
10. 𝄾 − 𝄾 𝄾 = ...

DIVISION

(Sample)

1. 𝄾 ÷ 2 = ...𝄾.... (See Lesson 6, Part 1, No. 2)
2. 𝄼 ÷ 4 = ...   ditto   9
3. 𝄾 ÷ 2 = ...   ,,   22
4. 𝄻 ÷ 2 = ...   ,,   1
5. 𝄻 ÷ 8 = ...   ,,   6
6. 𝄼 ÷ 8 = ...   ,,   2
7. 𝄾 ÷ 4 = ...   ,,   15
8. 𝄼 ÷ 16 = ...   ,,   4
9. 𝄻 ÷ 4 = ...   ,,   7
10. 𝄼 ÷ 2 = ...   ,,   3

EL 413

LESSON 8
The Dot

A dot after a note or rest increases its time value by one-half.

Part I

Write the values of each of the dotted notes and rests on the blank staffs. Study the samples.

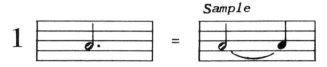

Part II

Write a single dotted note or rest that equals the various combinations.

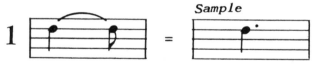

LESSON 9
Information Please
(Dotted Note and Rest Values)

Part I

DIRECTIONS: On each of the dotted lines, write the number which gives the correct amount of notes that are equal to the first part of each problem.

1. 𝅝. = ...3... 𝅗𝅥 *(Sample)*

2. 𝅝. = ... 𝅗𝅥

3. 𝅝. = ... ♪

4. 𝅝. = ... 𝅘𝅥𝅯

5. 𝅗𝅥. = ... 𝅗𝅥

6. 𝅗𝅥. = ... ♪

7. 𝅗𝅥. = ... 𝅘𝅥𝅯

8. 𝅗𝅥. = ... ♪

9. 𝅘𝅥. = ... 𝅘𝅥𝅯

10. ♪. = ... 𝅘𝅥𝅯

11. 2 𝅗𝅥. = ... 𝅗𝅥

12. 2 𝅗𝅥. = ... ♪

13. 2 𝅗𝅥. = ... 𝅘𝅥𝅯

14. 2 𝅗𝅥. = ... ♪

15. 3 𝅗𝅥. = ... ♪

16. 4 𝅗𝅥. = ... ♪

17. 2 𝅗𝅥. = ... 𝅘𝅥𝅯

18. 3 𝅗𝅥. = ... 𝅘𝅥𝅯

19. 4 𝅗𝅥. = ... ♪

20. 2 ♪. = ... 𝅘𝅥𝅯

21. 3 ♪. = ... 𝅘𝅥𝅯

22. 4 ♪. = ... ♪

23. 5 ♪. = ... 𝅘𝅥𝅯

24. 6 ♪. = ... 𝅘𝅥𝅯

Part II

DIRECTIONS: On each of the dotted lines, write the number which gives the correct amount of rests that are equal to the first part of each problem.

1. 𝄻. = ...6... 𝄽 *(Sample)*

2. 𝄻. = ... 𝄻

3. 𝄻. = ... 𝄾

4. 𝄻. = ... 𝄿

5. 𝄼. = ... 𝄾

6. 𝄼. = ... 𝄽

7. 𝄼. = ... 𝄿

8. 𝄽. = ... 𝄿

9. 𝄽. = ... 𝄾

10. 𝄾. = ... 𝄿

11. 2 𝄼. = ... 𝄿

12. 2 𝄼. = ... 𝄾

13. 2 𝄼. = ... 𝄽

14. 2 𝄽. = ... 𝄾

15. 4 𝄽. = ... 𝄾

16. 3 𝄽. = ... 𝄾

17. 3 𝄽. = ... 𝄿

18. 4 𝄽. = ... 𝄿

19. 2 𝄽. = ... 𝄿

20. 4 𝄾. = ... 𝄿

21. 6 𝄾. = ... 𝄿

22. 2 𝄾. = ... 𝄿

23. 5 𝄾. = ... 𝄿

24. 3 𝄾. = ... 𝄿

LESSON 10
Computing Mixed Note and Rest Values in Fourths

Printed music consists of a combination of notes and rests. In other words, notes are never used exclusively and neither are rests used entirely. The combination of notes and rests (sound and silence) is what makes up music. Therefore in this lesson, drill will be given on mixed note and rest values.

DIRECTIONS: Give the total of each of the following combinations in fourths.

Note: This is ONE dotted quarter note not three. More than one note head on a single stem does not increase the value.

EL 413

Teachers' Note: The unit of rhythm is the BEAT, not the measure. Measures are made up of groups of beats. Consequently the student should first have a thorough conception of the various combinations that make a beat. This will serve as a solid background for an understanding of measures which will be presented later.

LESSON 11
The Quarter as a Beat Unit

Music is divided into fixed units of time called BEATS. The QUARTER (note, rest or any equivalent combination) is the unit that most commonly receives a beat or count. Musical beats consist of a combination of notes and rests. In each of the samples, the total of the notes and rests added together equals a quarter. Hence, a wheel has been drawn around each of these beats.

DIRECTIONS: You are to draw wheels around all the beats on the following staffs. See that every beat totals one quarter and also put a small 1 at the beginning of each.

THINK: Four sixteenths make a quarter ($\frac{4}{16} = \frac{1}{4}$). In figuring each beat, count up to four sixteenths by placing commas above the notes and rests. Let one comma represent a sixteenth. In the samples, notice that each eighth note and rest has two commas because they are each worth two sixteenths. A wheel is drawn around every four commas.

LESSON 12
Quarter Length Beats Continued

DIRECTIONS: Draw wheels around the beats on the staffs below. See that every beat totals a quarter. Put a small 1 at the beginning of each beat. See samples for special cases. Notice that the second sample beat consists of the dot (which is worth an eighth) plus the eighth rest which makes a total of one quarter. The third sample (𝅗𝅥.) equals three quarters. Therefore three wheels have been placed around it and three numbers underneath it.

NOTE: When a note or rest gets two or more beats, draw as many wheels around it as it has beats, and write the total number of beats below it.

LESSON 13
Measure Subdividing

A measure is a group of beats marked off by a bar line. The number of beats in a measure is determined by the upper number of the time signature at the beginning of a piece.

$\dfrac{2}{4}$ means → Two beats per measure / Quarter gets a beat

$\dfrac{3}{4}$ means → Three beats per measure / Quarter gets a beat

DIRECTIONS: Draw wheels around each of the beats on the following staffs and insert bar lines where needed. Number the first beat, 1; the second, 2; etc.

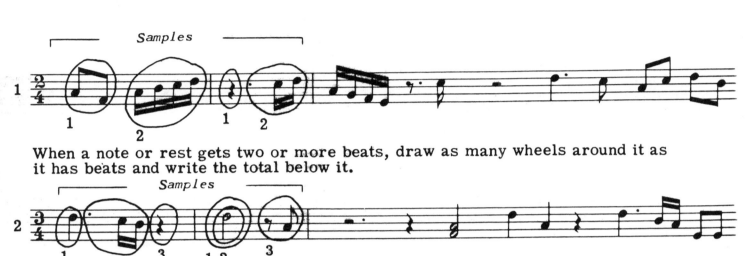

When a note or rest gets two or more beats, draw as many wheels around it as it has beats and write the total below it.

Always look at the time signature first!

LESSON 14
Measure Tailoring

DIRECTIONS: Blacken the note heads, add stems or flags to the notes on the staffs below. Do whatever is necessary to make each of the measures correct. When totaling the beats be sure to include the rest each time.

Always notice the time signature.

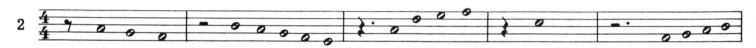

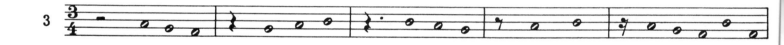

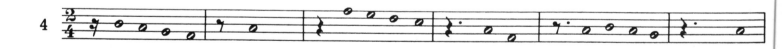

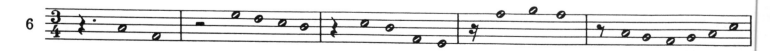

LESSON 15
Computing Mixed Note and Rest Values in Eighths

DIRECTIONS: Give the total of each of the following combinations in **EIGHTHS.**

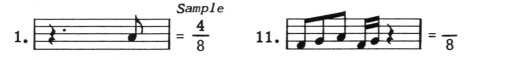

1. $= \dfrac{4}{8}$ (Sample)

2. $= \dfrac{}{8}$

3. $= \dfrac{}{8}$

4. $= \dfrac{}{8}$

5. $= \dfrac{}{8}$

6. $= \dfrac{}{8}$

7. $= \dfrac{}{8}$

8. $= \dfrac{4}{8}$

9. $= \dfrac{}{8}$

10. $= \dfrac{}{8}$

11. $= \dfrac{}{8}$

12. $= \dfrac{}{8}$

13. $= \dfrac{}{8}$

14. $= \dfrac{}{8}$

15. $= \dfrac{}{8}$

16. $= \dfrac{}{8}$

17. $= \dfrac{}{8}$

18. $= \dfrac{}{8}$

19. $= \dfrac{}{8}$

20. $= \dfrac{}{8}$

21. $= \dfrac{}{8}$

22. $= \dfrac{}{8}$

23. $= \dfrac{}{8}$

24. $= \dfrac{}{8}$

25. $= \dfrac{}{8}$

26. $= \dfrac{}{8}$

27. $= \dfrac{}{8}$

28. $= \dfrac{}{8}$

29. $= \dfrac{}{8}$

30. $= \dfrac{}{8}$

LESSON 16
Thirty-second Notes and Rests

A whole note (𝅝) may be divided into thirty-two parts, each part being a thirty-second note (𝅘𝅥𝅰).

Likewise a whole rest (▬) may be divided into thirty-two parts, each one being called a thirty-second rest (𝄿).

Part I (Notes)

DIRECTIONS: Beginning with line "b", write the correct number on each of the dotted lines. Be sure that the number is equal to the part before it and the part after it.

(Sample) a. 𝅝 = ...2... 𝅗𝅥 = ...4... 𝅘𝅥 = ...8... 𝅘𝅥𝅮 = ...16.. 𝅘𝅥𝅯 = ...32.. 𝅘𝅥𝅰

b. 𝅗𝅥 = ... 𝅘𝅥 = ... 𝅘𝅥𝅮 = ... 𝅘𝅥𝅯 = ... 𝅘𝅥𝅰

c. 𝅘𝅥 = ... 𝅘𝅥𝅮 = ... 𝅘𝅥𝅯 = ... 𝅘𝅥𝅰

d. 𝅘𝅥𝅮 = ... 𝅘𝅥𝅯 = ... 𝅘𝅥𝅰

e. 𝅘𝅥𝅯 = ... 𝅘𝅥𝅰

Part 2 (Rests)

Write the correct number on each of the dotted lines.

a. ▬ = ... ▬ = ... 𝄽 = ... 𝄾 = ... 𝄿 = ... 𝅀

b. ▬ = ... 𝄽 = ... 𝄾 = ... 𝄿 = ... 𝅀

c. 𝄽 = ... 𝄾 = ... 𝄿 = ... 𝅀

d. 𝄾 = ... 𝄿 = ... 𝅀

e. 𝄿 = ... 𝅀

Part 3 (Dotted Notes)

Write the correct number on each of the dotted lines.

a. 𝅝. = ... 𝅗𝅥 = ... 𝅘𝅥 = ... 𝅘𝅥𝅮 = ... 𝅘𝅥𝅯 = ... 𝅘𝅥𝅰

b. 𝅗𝅥. = ... 𝅘𝅥 = ... 𝅘𝅥𝅮 = ... 𝅘𝅥𝅯 = ... 𝅘𝅥𝅰

c. 𝅘𝅥. = ... 𝅘𝅥𝅮 = ... 𝅘𝅥𝅯 = ... 𝅘𝅥𝅰

d. 𝅘𝅥𝅮. = ... 𝅘𝅥𝅯 = ... 𝅘𝅥𝅰

e. 𝅘𝅥𝅯. = ... 𝅘𝅥𝅰

Part 4 (Dotted Rests)

Write the correct numbers.

a. ▬. = ... ▬ = ... 𝄽 = ... 𝄾 = ... 𝄿 = ... 𝅀

b. ▬. = ... 𝄽 = ... 𝄾 = ... 𝄿 = ... 𝅀

c. 𝄽. = ... 𝄾 = ... 𝄿 = ... 𝅀

d. 𝄾. = ... 𝄿 = ... 𝅀

e. 𝄿. = ... 𝅀

LESSON 17
Information Please
(Thirty-second Note and Rest Values)

Part I

DIRECTIONS: On each of the dotted lines, write a number giving the correct amount of notes or rests needed to equal the first part of each problem. Consult Lesson 16 whenever a question arises.

1. ♩ = ..16.. ♪ (Sample)
2. ♩ ♪ = ... ♪
3. 𝄽 = ... 𝄾
4. 𝅝 = ... ♪
5. ♩. = ... ♪
6. 𝄾 = ... 𝄾
7. 𝄻 = ... 𝄾
8. ♩. = ... ♪
9. 𝄼 = ... 𝄾
10. ♪ = ... ♪

11. ♪. = ... ♪
12. ♪. = ... ♪
13. 𝄾 = ... 𝄾
14. 𝄽. = ... 𝄾
15. ♩ = ... ♪
16. ♪ = ... ♪
17. 𝄾. = ... 𝄾
18. ♩ ♪ = ... ♪
19. ♪ ♪ = ... ♪
20. ♫ = ... ♪

21. 𝄼. = ... 𝄾
22. ♫ = ... ♪
23. 𝄾 𝄾 = ... 𝄾
24. 𝄾. = ... 𝄾
25. ♩. = ... ♪
26. 𝄽 𝄾 = ... 𝄾
27. ♩. ♪ = ... ♪
28. 𝄼 𝄾 = ... 𝄾
29. ♪ ♫ = ... ♪
30. ♪. = ... ♪

Part II

DIRECTIONS: On each of the dotted lines, write a number giving the correct amount of notes or rests needed to equal the first part of each problem.

Addition
1. ♪ + ♩ = ... ♪
2. ♩. + ♪ = ... ♪
3. 𝄾 + 𝄽 + 𝄾 = ... 𝄾
4. ♫ + ♫ = ... ♪
5. ♬♬ = ... ♪

Subtraction
6. ♩ - ♪ = ... ♪
7. ♪ - ♫ = ... ♪
8. 𝄼 - 𝄾𝄾 = ... 𝄾
9. ♪ - ♪ = ... ♪
10. 𝅝 - ♫ = ... ♪

Multipication
11. ♪ × 2 = ... ♪ (16ths)
12. ♪ × 6 = ... ♪
13. ♪ × 4 = ... ♪
14. ♪ × 8 = ... ♪
15. ♪ × 10 = ... ♪

EL 413

LESSON 18

The Eighth as the Beat Unit

The EIGHTH (note, rest, or any equal combination) is also used as a unit that receives a beat or count. In each of the samples, the total of the notes and rests added together equals an EIGHTH. Therefore a wheel has been drawn around each of these beats.

DIRECTIONS: Draw wheels around all the beats on the following staffs. See that each beat totals one EIGHTH. Put a small 1 at the beginning of each.

THINK: Four thirty-seconds make an eighth (4/32=1/8). In figuring each beat, count up to four thirty-seconds by placing commas above the notes and rests. Let one comma represent a thirty-second. In the samples, notice that each sixteenth has two commas because they are each worth two thirty-seconds. The dotted sixteenth has three commas because it is worth three thirty-seconds. A wheel is drawn around every four commas.

LESSON 19

Eighth Length Beats Continued

(Using dotted notes and rests, also multiple beat notes and rests)

DIRECTIONS: Draw wheels around the beats on the staffs below. See that every beat totals an eighth, and also put a small 1 at the beginning of each beat. See samples for special cases. Notice that the second sample beat consists of the dot (which is worth a sixteenth) plus the sixteenth rest which makes a total of one eighth. The third sample (♪.) equals three eighths; therefore, three wheels have been placed around it and three numbers underneath it.

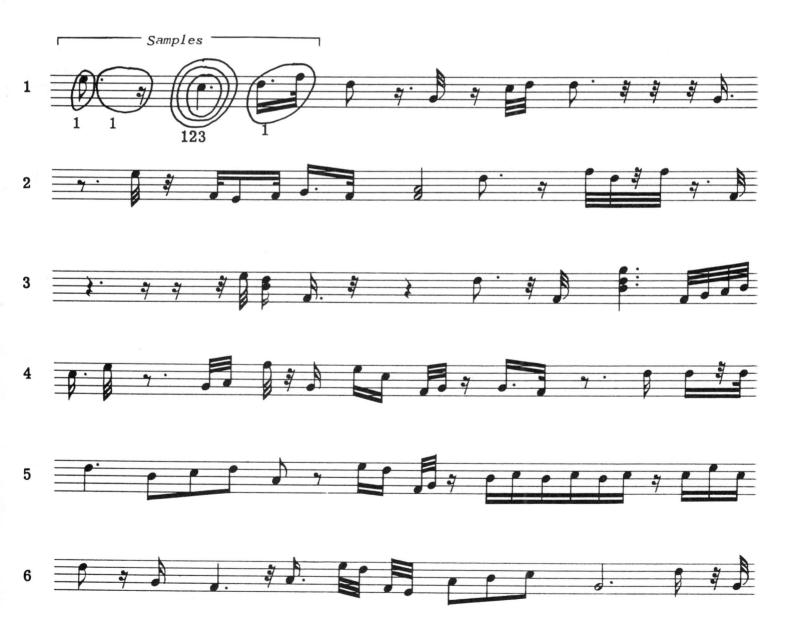

LESSON 20
Measures
(Eighth as a beat unit)

Six-eight () is the most widely used time signature having the eighth as a beat unit. However, 3/8, 9/8 and 12/8 are occasionally used.

DIRECTIONS: Draw wheels around each of the beats on the following staffs and insert bar lines where needed. Number the first beat, 1; the second, 2; etc. When a note or rest gets two or more beats, draw as many wheels around it as it has beats and write the total number of beats below it.

LESSON 21

Measure Tailoring

DIRECTIONS: Blacken the note heads, and add stems or flags to the notes on the staffs below. Do whatever is necessary to make each of the measures correct. When totaling the beats, be sure to include the rest each time.

LESSON 22
The Double Dot

One dot after a note or rest increases its time value by one half.

THE SECOND DOT AFTER A NOTE OR REST INCREASES THE TIME VALUE OF THE FIRST DOT BY ONE HALF.

Notice in the first sample (♪··) the first dot is worth an eighth and the second dot is worth half of the eighth or a sixteenth. In like manner, the second dot in the second sample is worth a quarter.

DIRECTIONS: In each of the squares below, you are to write a note or rest which is equal in value to the dot. Be sure to watch closely to see whether you are to give the value of the FIRST dot or the SECOND dot.

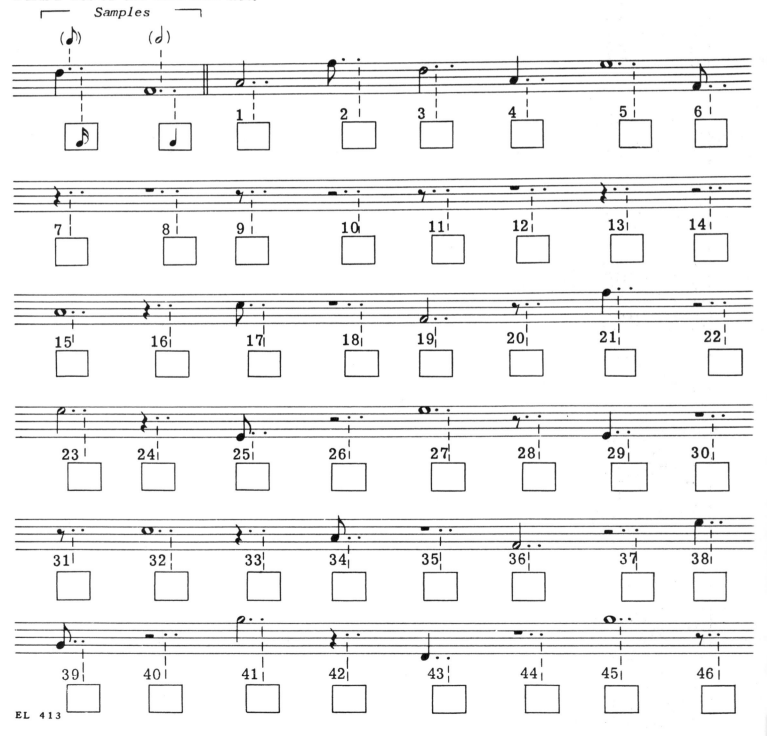

LESSON 23
Measure Subdividing
(The HALF as a Beat Unit)

Sometimes the HALF is used as a beat unit. It usually occurs in slower music such as hymns. Notice in the following signatures, a HALF gets a beat.

DIRECTIONS: Draw wheels around each of the beats on the following staffs and insert bar lines where needed. Number the first beat, 1; the second, 2; etc. When a note or rest gets two or more beats, draw as many wheels around it as it has beats and write the total number of beats below it.

LESSON 24
Triplets

So far, you have not divided notes into three equal parts. In order to do this, you would need THIRD notes. But instead of inventing a new kind of note (a third note) music writers have adopted the use of TRIPLETS. Triplets are a means of dividing a note into three equal parts. This is done by means of an italic three and a slur. For example, three half notes (♩♩♩) with an italic three joined by a slur no longer are half notes but collectively equal a whole note. Study the following triplet chart:

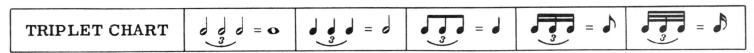

DIRECTIONS: You are to complete each of the measures below by converting the three notes into a TRIPLET. Insert the italic three and a slur, also blacken the note heads and add stems and flags wherever necessary.

THINK: First find out what ONE note is needed to complete the measure and write that note in the blank square above. Then convert the three notes into a triplet which equals the value of that one note. Consult the triplet chart whenever required.

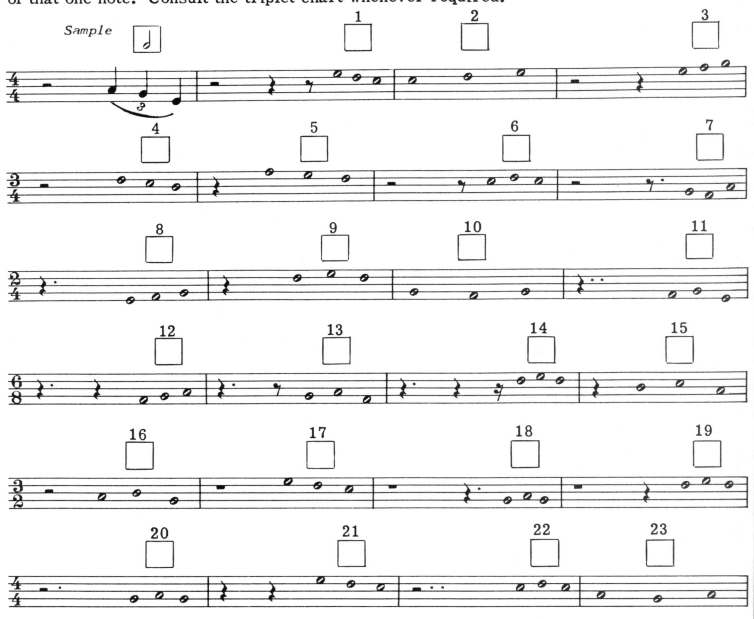

LESSON 25
Comparison of Beat Units

DIRECTIONS: In the squares below, write the number of beats that each of the following note and rest groups receives in the various time signatures indicated. The two half notes in the sample get 4 beats in 6/4 time; 8 beats in 12/8 time and 2 beats in 4/2 time.

#		6/4	12/8	4/2	#		6/4	12/8	4/2
1. (Sample)	=	4	8	2	11.	=			
2.	=				12.	=			
3.	=				13.	=			
4.	=				14.	=			
5.	=				15.	=			
6.	=				16.	=			
7.	=				17.	=			
8.	=				18.	=			
9.	=				19.	=			
10.	=				20.	=			

EL 413

LESSON 26
The Game of True and False

DIRECTIONS: Below are thirty statements about rhythm. If the statement is TRUE, mark T in the answer column. If it is FALSE, mark F. All the information has been presented in the preceding pages of this book. It is a good plan to review these pages.

Date _____   Grade marked _____

_____   _____
(Signature of student)   (Signature of teacher)

Answer
column

1. Four sixteenths equal one-half .... 1._____
2. Two half notes are as long as four quarter notes .... 2._____
3. An eighth less a sixteenth equals a sixteenth,................................... 3._____
4. A quarter plus an eighth equals six sixteenths.................................... 4._____
5. A half equals four sixteenths... 5._____
6. A quarter multiplied by four equals a whole...................................... 6._____
7. A quarter divided by four equals an eighth .... 7._____
8. A dotted quarter equals three eighths.. 8._____
9. A dotted half minus an eighth equals five eighths .... 9._____
10. Two dotted quarters equal three undotted quarters............................... 10._____
11. A dotted half divided by three equals an eighth .... 11._____
12. Six sixteenths equal three quarters .... 12._____
13. A dotted eighth plus a sixteenth equals one quarter .... 13._____
14. In four-four time, a quarter gets one beat...................................... 14._____
15. A quarter always gets one beat.. 15._____
16. In four-four time, a dotted half gets three beats .... 16._____
17. In three-four time, there are three beats to each rest .... 17._____
18. In two-four time, a half note makes a measure .... 18._____
19. The upper number of a time signature tells what kind of
      note gets one beat .... 19._____
20. A dotted eighth plus a sixteenth equals three eighths .... 20._____
21. Sixteen 32nds equal one-half .... 21._____
22. The dot after a sixteenth is worth a 32nd .... 22._____
23. In six-eight time, an eighth note makes a measure.............................. 23._____
24. In three-eight time, a quarter note gets two beats............................. 24._____
25. The second dot after a half, equals an eighth.................................. 25._____
26. In three-two time, a half note gets two beats.................................. 26._____
27. Three quarter notes joined by an italic three and a slur
      equal a half note .... 27._____
28. A whole note always gets four beats .... 28._____
29. A dotted quarter gets three beats in three-eight time .... 29._____
30. Six quarters make a measure in three-two time .... 30._____

JOHN W. SCHAUM RHYTHM SPELLER

How To Use The Rhythm Speller

The classical definition of music states that it consists of Melody, Rhythm, and Harmony. Not only is this an excellent definition, but it gives the logical sequence to be used in teaching the three elements.

At the outset of music study, the pupils learn tunes and pieces (melody). When his mental development increases, rhythmic understanding is taught. This doesn't mean that the pupil should not be taught rhythm earlier or that he should not play in rhythm from the very start. It means that the playing in rhythm at the beginning should be mainly by feeling rather than by intellectual comprehension. A mental grasp of rhythm implies a knowledge of fractions. In most public and private school, fractions are not presented until the fifth grade or when the child is approximately ten years old. It is at this point or later that the Rhythm Speller can be used most effectively. As a pre-requisite to the Rhythm Speller, the pupils should have had Theory Lesson I & II & III and Note Speller I & II by John W. Schaum or their equivalent.

This Rhythm Speller makes no attempt to teach the feeling of rhythm. That would require the guidance of a competent teacher. The Rhythm Speller does aim to present an understanding of note and rest values so that the student will be able to comprehend the raw materials that go to make rhythm. The pupil will learn the fractional values of notes, rests, beats, measures, etc. With this clarified mental concept, the rhythmic understanding will be awakened.

We do not teach pitch names because they have been amply treated in the other Schaum writing books.

We are convinced that if the pupil can do all the mathematical processes with notes and rests: i.e. add, subtract, multiply and divide: he then will understand counting and measure construction. It is this understanding that we undertake to teach in this speller. The feeling for rhythm is an intangible thing which can not be taught in print. In fact, there is a well known motto which says: "Rhythm is caught, not taught." That is true of the rhythmic feeling. But the mental grasp of rhythmic construction can be taught in print, and that is the goal of this book.

The Schaum Theory Lessons and Note Spellers have stressed pitch and staff recognition primarily and delayed fractional problems to conform with the pupil's mental readiness. It is for that reason that we now present this detailed and comprehensive rhythmic study as a follow-on to these first writing books.

ANSWER PAGE

IMPORTANT NOTE TO THE TEACHER

Please remove this sheet before the student begins the book. It is enclosed for convenience and expediency in correcting the lessons contained in the John W. Schaum Rhythm Speller, Book I.

Lesson 1
Part 1-a, One whole note. b, Two half notes. c, Four quarter notes. d, Eight eighth notes. e, Sixteen sixteenth notes. Part 2-a, One whole rest. b, Two half rests. c, Four quarter rests. d, Eight eighth rests. e, Sixteen sixteenth rests.

Lesson 2
1, Two half notes. 2, Four quarter notes. 3, Four quarter notes. 4, Sixteen sixteenth notes. 5, One whole note. 6, Eight eighth notes. 7, Two half notes. 8, Sixteen sixteenth notes. 9, Sixteen sixteenth notes. 10, Eight eighth notes. 11, One whole note.

Lesson 3
Part 1-1=2; 2=2; 3=8; 4=4; 5=16; 6=4; 7=4; 8=16; 9=8; 10=8; 11=2; 12=6; 13=8; 14=4; 15=4; 16=16; 17=12; 18=8; 19=2; 20=4; 21=10; 22=8; 23=6; 24=16; 25=14; 26=12; 27=1; 28=1; 29=1; 30=1; Part 2-1=2nd; 2=1st; 3=1st; 4=2nd; 5=2nd; 6=2nd; 7=1st; 8=2nd; 9=2nd; 10=1st; 11=2nd; 12=2nd; 13=2nd; 14=1st; 15=2nd.

Lesson 4
Addition: 1=1/2; 2=1/4; 3=whole; 4=1/4; 5=1/2; 6=1/8; 7=whole; 8=1/4; 9=whole; 10=1/2. Subtraction: 1=1/2; 2=1/8; 3=1/4; 4=1/8; 5=1/16; 6=1/2; 7=1/4; 8=1/4; 9=1/16; 10=1/8. Multiplication: 1=1/4; 2=whole; 3=1/2; 4=whole; 5=1/2; 6=1/8; 7=1/2; 8=whole; 9=1/4; 10=whole; Division; 1=1/8; 2=1/2; 3=1/4; 4=1/8; 5=1/16; 6=1/8; 7=1/4; 8=1/16; 9=1/16; 10=1/16.

Lesson 5
1, Eight 8th rests. 2, Sixteen 16th rests. 3, Eight 8th rests. 4, Sixteen 16th rests. 5, One whole rest. 6, Four quarter rests. 7, Two half rests. 8, Eight 8th rests. 9, Four quarter rests. 10, Sixteen 16th rests. 11, One whole rest.

Lesson 6
Part 1-1=2; 2=8; 3=2; 4=16; 5=4; 6=8; 7=4; 8=8; 9=4; 10=2; 11=16; 12=6; 13=4; 14=8; 15=4; 16=12; 17=16; 18=8; 19=4; 20=8; 21=12; 22=2; 23=10; 24=6; 25=16; 26=14; 27=1; 28=1; 29=1; 30=1. Part 2-1=2nd; 2=2nd; 3=2nd; 4=2nd; 5=1st; 6=2nd; 7=1st; 8=2nd; 9=1st; 10=2nd; 11=2nd; 12=1st; 13=2nd; 14=1st; 15=1st.

Lesson 7
Addition: 1=whole; 2=1/2; 3=1/8; 4=1/2; 5=whole; 6=1/4; 7=whole; 8=whole; 9=1/2; 10=1/4. Subtraction: 1=1/8; 2=1/2; 3=1/4; 4=1/8; 5=1/2; 6=1/16; 7=1/8; 8=1/4; 9=1/4; 10=1/16; Multiplication: 1=1/2; 2=whole; 3=whole; 4=1/8; 5=1/2; 6=whole; 7=1/4; 8=1/4; 9=whole; 10=1/2. Division: 1=1/8; 2=1/4; 3=1/16; 4=1/4; 5=1/16; 6=1/8; 7=1/16; 8=1/16; 9=1/8; 10=1/2.

Lesson 8
Part 1-1, 1/2 & 1/4 tied. 2, 1/4 & 1/8 rest. 3, 1/4 & note tied. 4, 1/8 & 1/16 rest. 5, whole & 1/2 note 6, 1/8 & 1/16 note tied. 7, whole & 1/2 rest. 8, 1/2 & note tied. 9, 1/2 & 1/4 rest. 10, 1/4 & 1/8 rest. Par 1, dotted 1/4. 2, dotted whole. 3, dotted 1/2. 4, do whole. 5, dotted 1/4. 6, dotted 1/4. 7, dotted 1/2. 8, do 1/8. 9, dotted 1/8. 10, dotted whole.

Lesson 9
Part 1-1=3; 2=6; 3=12; 4=24; 5=3; 6=6; 7=12; 8=3; 10=3; 11=6; 12=12; 13=24; 14=6; 15=9; 16=12; 17=12; 18 19=24; 20=6; 21=9; 22=12; 23=15; 24=18. Part 2-1=6; 3=12; 4=24; 5=6; 6=3; 7=12; 8=6; 9=3; 10=3; 11=24; 12 13=6; 14=6; 15=12; 16=9; 17=18; 18=24; 19=12; 20=12; 21 22=6; 23=15; 24=9.

Lesson 10
1=3/4; 2=2/4; 3=3/4; 4=3/4; 5=5/4; 6=4/4; 7=6/4; 8= 9=1/4; 10=1/4; 11=6/4; 12=4/4; 13=2/4; 14=3/4; 15= 16=2/4; 17=2/4; 18=6/4; 19=3/4; 20=3/4; 21=3/4; 22= 23=7/4; 24=2/4; 25=3/4; 26=4/4; 27=4/4; 28=3/4; 29= 30=5/4.

Lesson 11
Staff No. 1:-First wheel after samples=16th + 8th + 1 second=four 16ths; third=two 8ths; fourth=quarter; fi two 16ths + one 8th; sixth=16th + 8th + 16th. Staff No First wheel=16th + 8th + 16th; second=one 8th + two 16 third=16th + 8th + 16th; fourth=one 8th + two 16ths; f two 16ths + one 8th; sixth=16th + 8th + 16th; seventh 8th + two 16ths; eighth=one 8th + two 16ths. Staff No. First wheel=two 16ths + one 8th; second=four 16ths; th four 16ths; fourth=two 16ths + one 8th; fifth=quar sixth=four 16ths; seventh=one 8th + two 16ths; eighth 16ths + one 8th. Staff No. 4:-First=16th + 8th + second=quarter; third=two 8ths; fourth=8th + two 16 fifth=16th + 8th + 16th; sixth=one 8th + two 16ths; seve two 8ths; eighth=two 16ths + one 8th; ninth=four 16 Staff No. 5:-First=four 16ths; second=16th + 8th + 1 third=two 8ths; fourth=16th + 8th + 16th; fifth=one 8 two 16ths; sixth=one 8th + two 16ths; seventh= 16 8th + 16th. Staff No. 6: - First=four 16ths; second 16ths + one 8th; third=four 16ths; fourth=four 16ths; f quarter; sixth=one 8th + two 16ths; seventh=two 8 eighth=one 8th + two 16ths.

Lesson 12
Staff No. 1:-First wheel after samples=16th + dotted second=four wheels around the whole note; third=quar fourth=dot + two 16ths; fifth=two 8ths; sixth=quarter; enth=8th + two 16ths. Staff No. 2:-First=four wh around whole rest; second=two 16ths + one 8th; third=

Lesson 12 (con't.)

8th + 16th; fourth=16th + dotted 8th; fifth = quarter; [sixt]h=dot + 8th; seventh=quarter; eighth=dot + two 16ths; [nint]h=quarter; tenth=dot + 8th; eleventh=16th + dotted 8th. [Staf]f No. 3:-First=dotted 8th + 16th; second=two wheels [arou]nd half rest; third=quarter; fourth=dot + two 16ths; [fift]h=three wheels around dotted half; sixth=dotted 8th + [16th]; seventh=quarter; eighth=dot + two 16ths; ninth=two [16th]s + 8th; tenth=two 8ths. Staff No. 4:-First=16th + [dott]ed 8th; second=quarter; third=dot + two 16ths; fourth= [two]16ths; fifth=dotted 8th + 16th; sixth=quarter; seventh= [dot]+ 8th; eighth=quarter; ninth=dot + two 16ths; tenth= [thre]e wheels around dotted half rest. Staff No. 5:-First= [two]16ths; second=quarter; third=two wheels around half; [four]th=quarter; fifth=dot + two 16ths; sixth=four 16ths; [seve]nth=four wheels around whole; eighth=quarter; ninth= [dot]+ 8th; tenth=two 16ths + 8th. Staff No. 6:- First= [16th]+ 8th + 16th; second=quarter; third=dot + two 16ths; [four]th =four wheels around whole rest; fifth=8th + two [16th]s; sixth=16th + dotted 8th; seventh=quarter; eighth= [dot]+ two 16ths; ninth=8th + two 16ths; tenth=dotted 8th + [16th].

Lesson 13

[Staf]f No. 1:-First measure after samples=four 16ths + [dott]ed 8th + 16th; second measure=half; third=dotted quar- [ter]+ 8th; fourth=four 8ths. Staff No. 2:-First measure [afte]r samples=dotted half; second=quarter + half; third= [thre]e quarters; fourth=dotted quarter + two 16ths + two [8ths]. Staff No. 3:-First measure=two 8ths + dotted 8th + [16th]; second=four 8ths; third=half; fourth=two quarters; [fift]h=four 8ths; sixth=dotted quarter + two 16ths. Staff [No.]4:-First measure=dotted half; second=half + quarter; [thir]d=four 8ths + quarter; fourth=two 8ths + two quarters; [fift]h=dotted quarter + 8th + quarter; sixth=quarter + two [8ths]+ quarter; seventh=three quarters. Staff No.5:-First [mea]sure=two 16ths + 8th + two 16ths + 8th + four 16ths + [quar]ter; second=half + dotted 8th + 16th + quarter; third= [who]le; fourth =dotted quarter + 8th + quarter + dotted [8th]+ 16th; fifth=whole. Staff No. 6:-First measure=two [quar]ters + half; second=quarter + two 8ths + dotted quar- [ter]+ 8th; third=half + two quarters; fourth=dotted 8th + [16th]+ dotted half; fifth=8th + two 16ths + dotted quar- [ter]+ two 16ths + quarter.

Lesson 14

[The]following answers provide the note value names only. [Dot]s or dotted rests are not mentioned for purposes of [cond]ensation. Only one answer is given here yet in some [case]s there could be other correct answers. The teacher [will]have to accept these as long as the measure total is [corr]ect. Staff No. 1:-Second measure=8th two 16ths; [third]=8th + quarter; fourth=16th + 8th + quarter; fifth= [half]+ two 8ths; sixth=three 8ths. Staff No. 2:- First [mea]sure=8th + quarter + half; second=four 16ths + quar- [ter]third=two 16ths + two quarters; fourth=dotted half; [fifth]=four 16ths. Staff No. 3:-First measure=8th + two [16th]s; second=two 8ths + quarter; third=two 16ths + quar- [ter]fourth=eighth + half; fifth=three 16ths + two quarters. [Staff]No. 4:-First measure=three 16ths + quarter; second= [dotte]d quarter; third=four 16ths; fourth=two 16ths; fifth= [half]+ 8th + two 16ths; sixth=8th. Staff No. 5:- First [mea]sure=quarter + two 8ths; second=two 16ths + quar= [ter]+ half; third=8th + two 16ths + half; fourth=8th + two

Lesson 14 (con't.)

quarters; fifth=8th + two 16ths. Staff No. 6:-First measure=8th + quarter; second=four 16ths; third=8th + two 16ths + quarter; fourth=16th + 8th + half; fifth=8th + four 16ths + quarter.

Lesson 15

1=4; 2=4; 3=7; 4=7; 5=2; 6=5; 7=10; 8=2; 9=5; 10=8; 11=6; 12=4; 13=5; 14=5; 15=4; 16=11; 17=5; 18=3; 19=6; 20=8; 21=5; 22=3; 23=6; 24=4; 25=2; 26=3; 27=6; 28=8; 29=13; 30=4.

Lesson 16

Part 1:- b, 1/2=2/4=4/8=8/16=16/32; c, 1/4=2/8=4/16= 8/32; d, 1/8=2/16=4/32; e, 1/16=2/32. Part 2 - same answers for each line as part one. Part 3:-a, dotted whole=3/2=6/4=12/8=24/16=48/32; b,dotted 1/2=3/4=6/8= 12/16=24/32; c, dotted 1/4=3/8=6/16=12/32; d,dotted 1/8= 3/16=6/32; e, dotted 1/16=3/32. Part 4:-same answers for each line as part three.

Lesson 17

Part 1:-1=16; 2=12; 3=8; 4=32; 5=12; 6=4; 7=32; 8=24; 9=16; 10=2; 11=6; 12=3; 13=2; 14=12; 15=8; 16=4; 17=6; 18=20; 19=6; 20=4; 21=24; 22=8; 23=6; 24=3; 25=8; 26=10; 27=16; 28=20; 29=8; 30=3. Part 2:-Addition-1=10; 2=16; 3=14; 4=12; 5=8. Subtraction:-6=7; 7=2; 8=14; 9=1; 10=30. Multi- plication:-11=1; 12=3; 13=2; 14=4; 15=5.

Lesson 18

Staff No. 1:-First wheel after samples=16th + two 32nds; second wheel=32nd + 16th + 32nd; third=16th + two 32nds; fourth=32nd + 16th + 32nd; fifth=16th + two 32nds; sixth=two 32nds + 16th. Staff No. 2:-First wheel=two 32nds + 16th; second=two 32nds + 16th; third=two 32nds + 16th; fourth= four 32nds; fifth=32nd + 16th + 32nd; sixth=four 32nds; seventh=8th; eighth=four 32nds. Staff No. 3:-First wheel= 16th + two 32nds; second=two 32nds + 16th; third=32nd + 16th + 32nd; fourth=8th; fifth=two 16ths; sixth=16th + two 32nds; seventh =32nd + 16th + 32nd; eighth =16th + two 32nds; ninth=two 16ths. Staff No. 4:-First=two 32nds + 16th; second=four 32nds; third=four 32nds; fourth=32nd+ 16th + 32nd; fifth=two 16ths; sixth=32nd + 16th + 32nd; seventh=16th + two 32nds; eighth=two 16ths. Staff No. 5:- First wheel=four 32nds; second=two 32nds + 16th; third= four 32nds;fourth=four 32nds;fifth=eighth;sixth=two 16ths; seventh=two 32nds + 16th; eighth=two 16ths. Staff No. 6:= First wheel=32nd + 16th + 32nd; second=two 16ths; third= two 32nds + 16th; fourth=32nd + 16th + 32nd; fifth=four 32nds;sixth=four 32nds; seventh=16th + two 32nds; eighth= two 32nds + 16th.

Lesson 19

Staff No. 1:-First wheel after samples=8th; second=dotted 16th + 32nd; third=16th + two 32nds; fourth=8th; fifth = dot + two 32nds; sixth=32nd + dotted 16th. Staff No. 2:- First wheel=8th; second=dot + two 32nds; third=32nd + 16th + 32nd; fourth=dotted 16th + 32nd; fifth=four wheels around half; sixth=8th; seventh=dot + 16th; eighth=four

Lesson 19 (con't.)

32nds; ninth=dotted 16th + 32nd. Staff No. 3:-First=three wheels around dotted quarter;second=two 16ths; third=two 32nds + 16th; fourth=dotted 16th + 32nd; fifth =two wheels around quarter;sixth=8th;seventh=dot + two 32nds; eighth=three wheels around dotted quarter; ninth =four 32nds. Staff No. 4:-First wheel=dotted 16th + 32nd; sec-one=8th; third=dot + two 32nds; fourth=two 32nds + 16th; fifth=two 16ths; sixth=two 32nds + 16th; seventh=dotted 16th + 32nd; eighth=8th; ninth=dot + 16th; tenth=16th + two 32nds. Staff No. 5:- First=three wheels around dotted quarter; second = 8th; third = 8th; fourth = 8th; fifth =8th; sixth=8th; seventh=two 16ths; eighth=two 32nds + 16th; ninth=two 16ths; tenth = two 16ths; eleventh = two 16ths; twelfth=two 16ths; thirteenth=two 16ths. Staff No. 6:- First wheel=8th; second=two 16ths; third=three wheels around dotted quarter; fourth=32nd + dotted 16th; fifth= four 32nds; sixth=8th; seventh=8th; eighth=8th; ninth=six wheels around dotted half; tenth=16th + two 32nds.

Lesson 20

Staff No. 1:-First measure after samples=two 16ths + quarter + dotted quarter; second = dotted 8th + 16th + 8th + dotted quarter; third=dotted quarter + dotted quar- ter. Staff No. 2:-First measure=two 16ths + two 8ths; second=dotted quarter;third=four 32nds + quarter;fourth= dotted 8th + 16th + 8th; fifth=three 8ths; sixth=8th + quar- ter; seventh = quarter + 8th. Staff No. 3:-First = three 8ths + quarter + 8th; six 16ths + 8th + four 16ths; third= four 16ths + three 8ths + two 16ths. Staff No. 4:-First measure=quarter + two 16ths + four 32nds + 8th + two 16ths + dotted quarter; second = 8th + two 16ths + two 8ths + four 16ths + two 16ths + quarter. Staff No. 5:-First measure=dotted 8th + three 16th + dotted 8th + 16th + 8th; second=two 32nds + 16th + quarter + three 8ths; third= four 16ths + 8th + quarter + 8th. Staff No. 6:-First meas- ure=four 16ths + 8th; second=four 32nds + quarter; third= two 32nds + 16th + two 8ths; fourth=quarter + two 16ths; fifth=8th + two 16ths + 8th.

Lesson 21

The following answers provide the note value names only. Rests or dotted rests are not mentioned for purposes of condensation. Only one answer is given here, yet in some cases there could be other correct answers. The teacher will have to accept these as long as the measure total is correct. Staff No. 1:-Second measure=8th + quarter + 8th;third=quarter + three 8ths;fourth=quarter;fifth=dot- ted quarter; sixth=8th + dotted quarter. Staff No. 2:-First= quarter + three 8ths; second=two 16ths + 8th + half;third= 16th + quarter + two 8ths + two quarters;fourth=8th + two 16ths + quarter + half. Staff No.3:-First=16th + two quar- ters;second=16th + three 8ths + quarter; third=8th + quar- ter;fourth=four 16ths;fifth=8th + half. Staff No. 4:-First= two 16ths;second=16th + quarter;third=three 32nd + quar- ter;fourth=two 16ths + 8th;fifth=three 16ths. Staff No. 5:- First=16th + 8th + two quarters; second=four 32nds + quarter; third=two 16ths + 8th; fourth=16th + two 8ths + quarter. Staff No. 6:-First measure=16th + 8th; second= three 16ths + 8th;third=8th; fourth=16th + two 8ths;fifth= four 32nds.

Lesson 22

1=1/4; 2=1/32; 3=1/4; 4=1/8; 5=1/4; 6=1/16; 7=1/8; 8= 9=1/16; 10=1/8; 11=1/32; 12=1/2; 13=1/16; 14=1/4; 1/2; 16=1/16; 17=1/32; 18=1/4;19=1/4; 20=1/16; 21= 22=1/8; 23=1/8; 24=1/8; 25=1/16; 26=1/4; 27=1/4; 1/32; 29=1/16;30=1/2;31=1/16; 32=1/4; 33=1/16; 34=1 35=1/2;36=1/4; 37=1/8;38=1/8; 39=1/32; 40=1/4; 41= 42=1/8; 43=1/16; 44=1/4; 45=1/2; 46=1/32.

Lesson 23

Staff No. 1:-First measure after sample=2/8 + 1/4 + second=1/4 + 4/16 + 1/4 + 1/8 + 2/16 + 1/2; third=dc whole; fourth=4/4 + 1/2. Staff No. 2:-First measu 1/1 + 1/2 + 2/4; second=double dotted whole + 2/8; th 1/4 + 4/16 + dotted whole; fourth=dotted quarter + 1/ double dotted half + 3/8 + 1/4. Staff No. 3:-First me ure=4/8 + 1/2; second=2/4 + 1/2; third=double dotted + 2/16;fourth=4/8 + 2/4;fifth=dotted quarter + 1/8 + + 1/4. Staff No. 4:-First measure=1/4 + 2/8 + 1/1; ond=1/2 + 1/1;third=2/8 + 1/4 + dotted half + 1/4;fou double dotted half + 5/8; fifth=4/16 + 1/4 + 1/2 + Staff No. 5:-First measure=1/1 + 2/8 + 3/4; second + 1/2 + 2/8 + 1/4;third=double dotted whole + 1/4;fou 1/2 + 4/8 + double dotted half + 1/8. Staff No.6:-Fi measure=2/4 + 2/8 + 1/4; second=2/8 + 1/4 + 1/2; th double dotted half + 1/8; fourth=whole;fifth=whole; si 2/16 + 1/8 + 2/4 + 4/16.

Lesson 24

Each answer contains two fractions: the first repres the note in the square, the second represents the kin notes in the triplet 1, 1/8=3/16; 2, 1/1=3/2; 3, 1/4= 4, 1/4=3/8; 5, 1/2=3/4; 6, 1/8=3/16; 7, 1/16=3/32; 8, 3/16; 9, 1/4=3/8; 10, 1/2=3/4; 11, 1/16=3/32; 12, 3/16; 13, 1/4=3/8; 14, 1/16=3/32; 15, 1/2=3/4; 16, 1/ 17, 1/2=3/4; 18, 1/8=3/16; 19, 1/4=3/8; 20, 1/4=3/ 1/2=3/4; 22, 1/8=3/16; 23, 1/1=3/2.

Lesson 25

(1) illustrated (2) 2-4-1 (3) 4-8-2 (4) 6-12-3 (5) 2- (6) 2-4-1 (7) 6-12-3 (8) 2-4-1 (9) 6-12-3 (10) 4-8-2 4-8-2 (12) 2-4-1 (13) 2-4-1 (14) 6-12-3 (15) 4-8-2 (16 8-2 (17) 4-8-2 (18) 4-8-2 (19) 2-4-1 (20) 2-4-1.

Lesson 26

1=F; 2=T; 3=T; 4=T; 5=F; 6=T; 7=F; 8=T; 9=T; 10=T; 11 12=F; 13=T; 14=T; 15=F; 16=T; 17=F; 18=T; 19=F; 20 21=T; 22=T; 23=F; 24=T; 25=T; 26=F; 27=T; 28=F; 29 20=T.